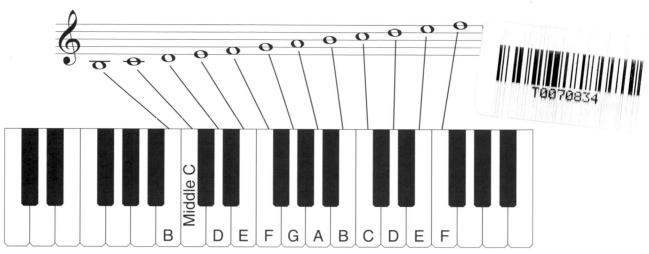

PLAYING YOUR KEYBOARD

Accompaniment Keys

The keys on the left side of your keyboard will play the accompaniment notes. Use your left hand to play these notes. Apply the UNCOLORED stickers on these keys as shown in the picture.

Melody Keys

The melody keys start on Middle C and move to the right. Use your right hand to play these keys. Apply the colored stickers to these keys as shown in the picture.

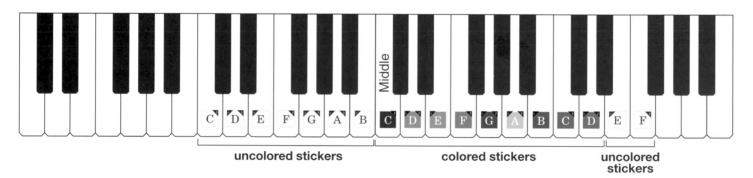

Middle C is a reference point found in most of the songs in this book. Once you've found Middle C, you'll know you're playing the melody in the correct place. Locating Middle C depends on the kind of keyboard you have.

> Acoustic Pianos: To find Middle C, look for the brand name, usually in the middle of the piano directly above the keys. The C just below the brand name is Middle C, right in the middle of the keyboard.

> Electronic Keyboards and Digital Pianos: Generally Middle C is the first C to the right of the chord keys. Many electronic keyboards are different. The best way to identify your chord keys and Middle C is to consult your owner's manual.

HOW TO READ E-Z PLAY® NOTATION
Color Coding
Each melody note has a specific color. To play each song, match the color on the music (under each note on the staff) with the color of the keyboard sticker. Each note is also named by letter. If you know the letter names of the keys you can also read the music in this way.

Optional Harmony or Chord Accompaniment
The uncolored stickers can be applied below Middle C if you wish. You can use your left hand to play harmony or an accompaniment by playing the note named in the box above the melody. Hold down the left-hand note indicated until another letter appears. If your keyboard has chord accompaniment keys or buttons, you can use these in the same way.

Instrument Settings
An instrument setting is indicated for each song. This is just a suggestion and ANY instrument setting can be used. Be creative!

Rhythm Settings
A rhythm setting is indicated for each song. If a song has a 3 at the beginning, use the Waltz setting. However, if there is a 4 at the beginning, Rock, Swing, or any other rhythm can be used, even if only one rhythm is suggested.

COUNTING BEATS AND RHYTHMS
All songs use different types of **notes** to represent long and short sounds. Each note relates to the beat, the steady rhythmic pulse of the music.

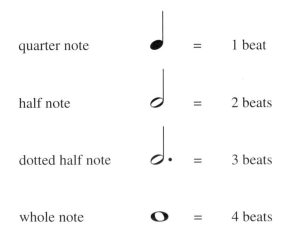

The quarter note can be divided.

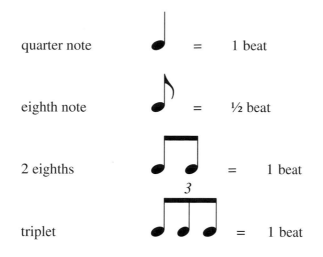

quarter note	=	1 beat
eighth note	=	½ beat
2 eighths	=	1 beat
triplet	=	1 beat

Rests are used to indicate silence, or when not to play. There is a rest to match each note value.

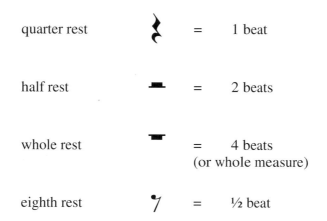

quarter rest	=	1 beat
half rest	=	2 beats
whole rest	=	4 beats (or whole measure)
eighth rest	=	½ beat

BAR LINES AND TIME SIGNATURES

To make reading easier, the staff is divided by **bar lines** into equal segments called **measures**. A **double bar** is placed at the end of the song.

A **time signature** is placed at the beginning of every song. The top number of the time signature tells you how many beats are in each measure. So, for example, if the top number is 4, there are 4 beats in every measure.

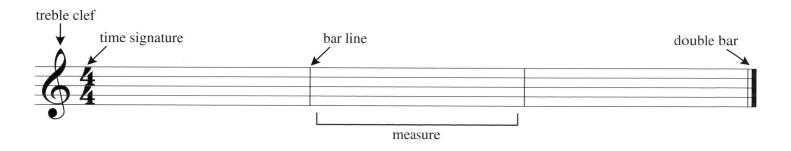

SHARPS, FLATS, AND NATURALS

A **sharp** sign ♯ raises the pitch of a note a half-step. On the keyboard, a sharp is usually played on a black key.

For example, C♯ is the black key between C and D. F♯ is the black key between F and G.

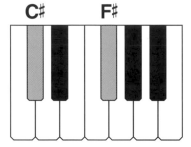

A **flat** sign ♭ lowers a pitch a half-step. Flats are usually played on the black keys. On the keyboard, B♭ is the black key between B and A. E♭ is between E and D.

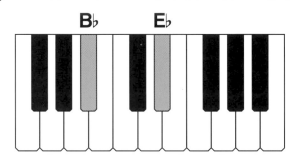

Sharps and flats stay sharp or flat for an entire measure, unless you see a **natural** sign: ♮

The natural sign **cancels** a sharp or flat.

MORE MUSICAL SIGNS AND SYMBOLS

Ties

A curved line connecting two notes with the same pitch is called a **tie**.

It "ties" the two notes together. The first note is played and counted for its full value, plus the value of the note it's tied to. The tied note is not played again. That's why there's not a letter inside the second note. A tie gives the note a longer value.

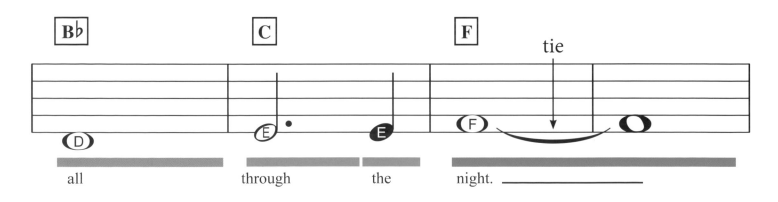

Repeat Sign

A **repeat sign** directs you to repeat a song, or part of a song. When you come to the two dots of the sign, go back and play that portion of the music again.

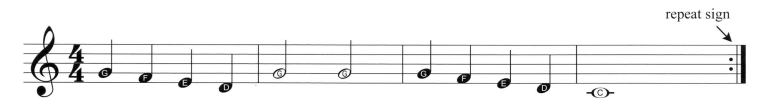

1st and 2nd Ending

In addition to a repeat sign, sometimes a **1st and 2nd ending signs** will be used. Play the repeated section as indicated, but instead of repeating the measure marked with the 1st ending, skip ahead to the measure marked 2nd ending, continuing on to the end of the song. This sign is often used when there is more than one verse in a song.

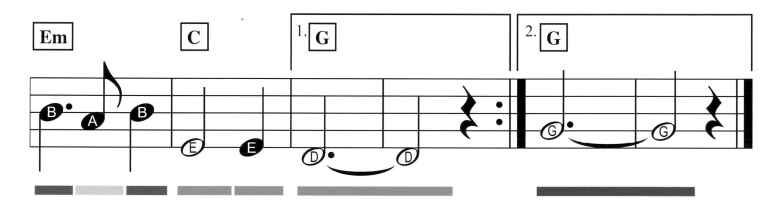

ALL THROUGH THE NIGHT

Welsh Folksong

Registration 1
Rhythm: Ballad

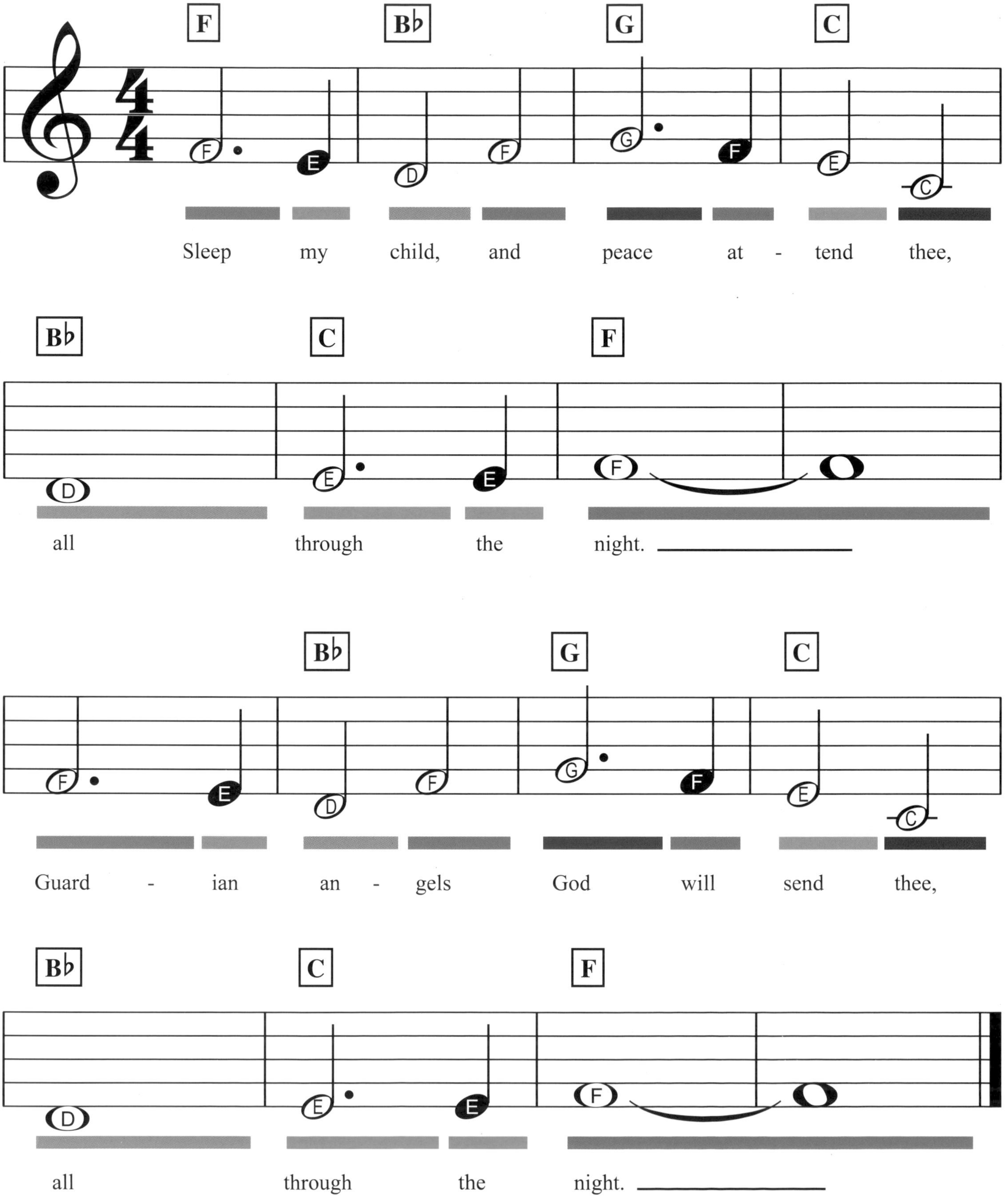

Sleep my child, and peace at - tend thee,

all through the night.

Guard - ian an - gels God will send thee,

all through the night.

BEAUTIFUL BROWN EYES

Traditional

Registration 1
Rhythm: Waltz

BANANA BOAT SONG

Jamaican Work Song

Registration 4
Rhythm: Calypso

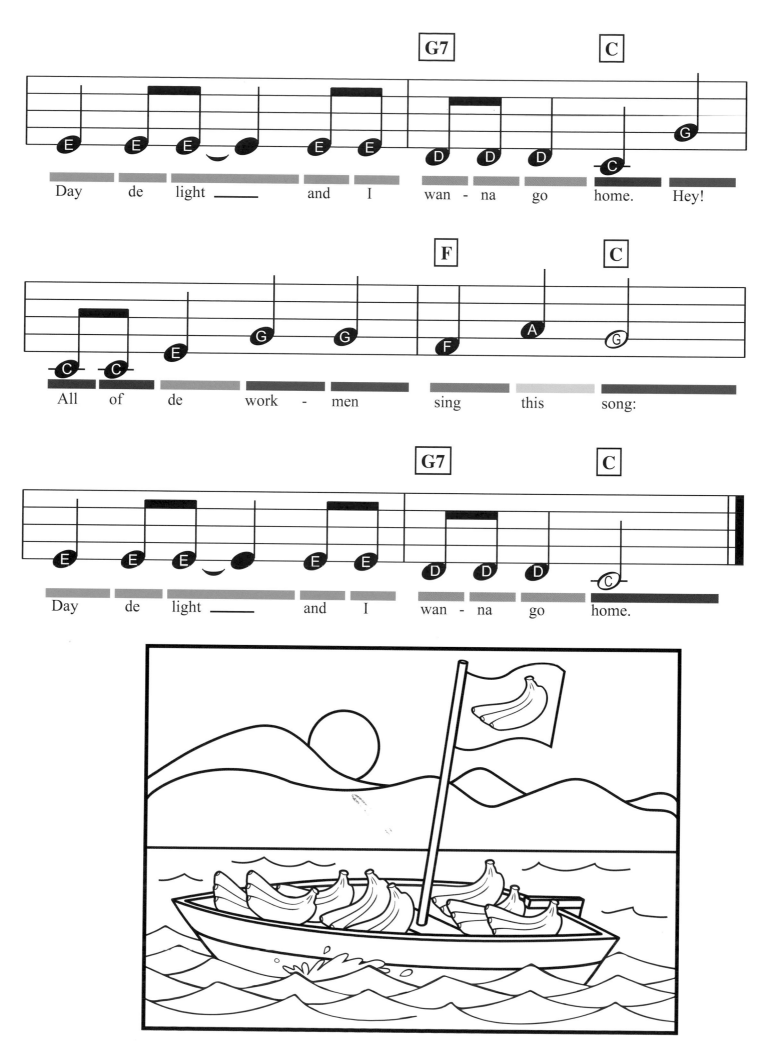

A BICYCLE BUILT FOR TWO
(Daisy Bell)

Registration 8
Rhythm: Waltz

Words and Music by
Harry Dacre

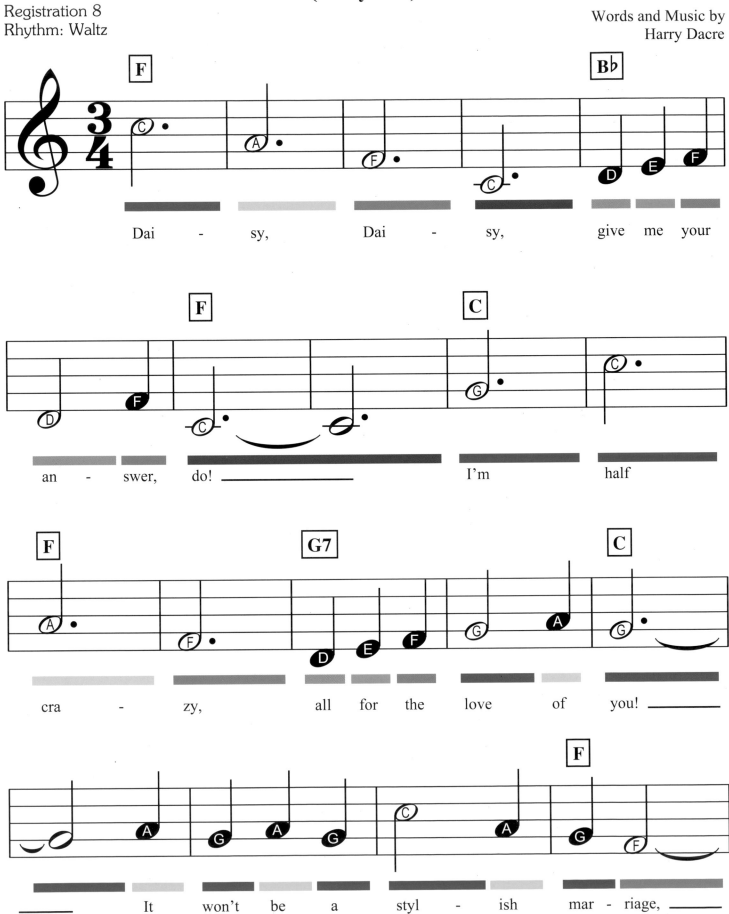

CAMPTOWN RACES

Registration 2
Rhythm: March

Words and Music by
Stephen C. Foster

ACROSS

5. This is a _____ note.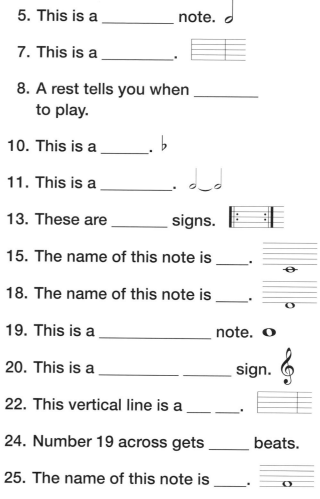

7. This is a _____.

8. A rest tells you when _____ to play.

10. This is a _____. ♭

11. This is a _____.

13. These are _____ signs.

15. The name of this note is ____.

18. The name of this note is ____.

19. This is a _____ note. 𝅝

20. This is a _____ _____ sign.

22. This vertical line is a ___ ___.

24. Number 19 across gets _____ beats.

25. The name of this note is ____.

DOWN

1. The first letter of the musical alphabet is _____.

2. This is a _____. ♯

3. This is a quarter _____.

4. This is a _____ note.

6. Music is _____ and easy to play.

9. A quarter note gets _____ beat.

12. The name of this note is ____.

14. A dotted half note gets _____ beats.

16. A half note gets _____ beats.

17. This is a _____ _____ note.

21. The name of this note is ____.

23. The name of this note is ____.

(Answers are on page 78.)

16

BILLY BOY

Traditional English Folksong

Registration 4
Rhythm: Swing or Fox Trot

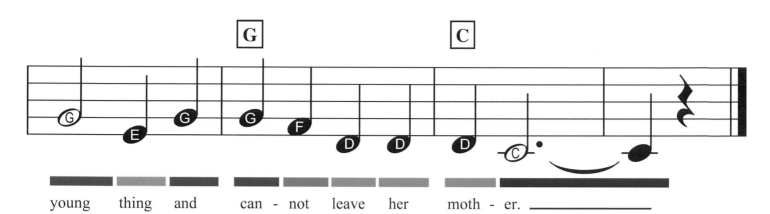

young   thing   and   can - not   leave   her   moth - er. _____

2. Can she bake a cherry pie...
   She can bake a cherry pie,
   Quick as you can wink your eye...

3. Oh, where does she live...
   She lives on the hill,
   Forty miles from the mill...

4. Did she bid you come in...
   Yes, she bade me to come in,
   And to kiss her on the chin...

5. And did she take your hat...
   Oh yes, she took my hat,
   And she threw it at the cat...

6. Did she set for you a chair...
   Yes, she set for me a chair,
   But the bottom wasn't there...

7. Can she make a feather bed...
   She can make a feather bed,
   That will rise above your head...

CAN-CAN
from ORPHEUS IN THE UNDERWORLD

By Jacques Offenbach

Registration 7
Rhythm: Polka or March

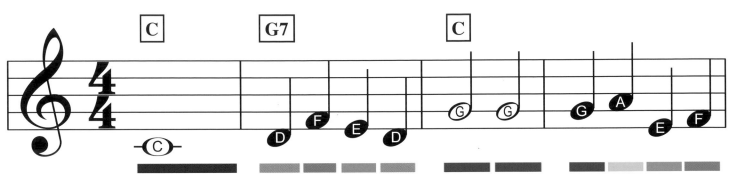

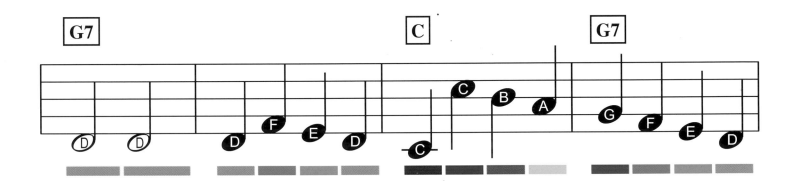

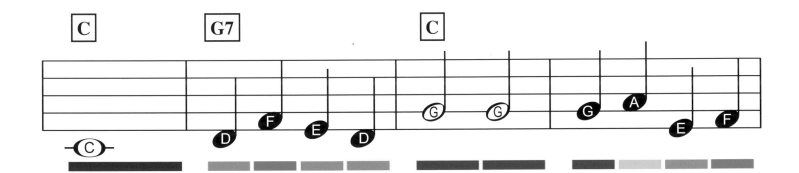

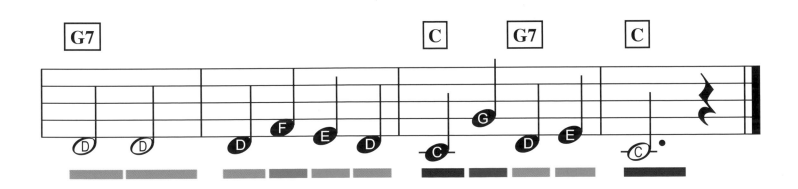

THE FARMER IN THE DELL

Traditional

Registration 9
Rhythm: Waltz

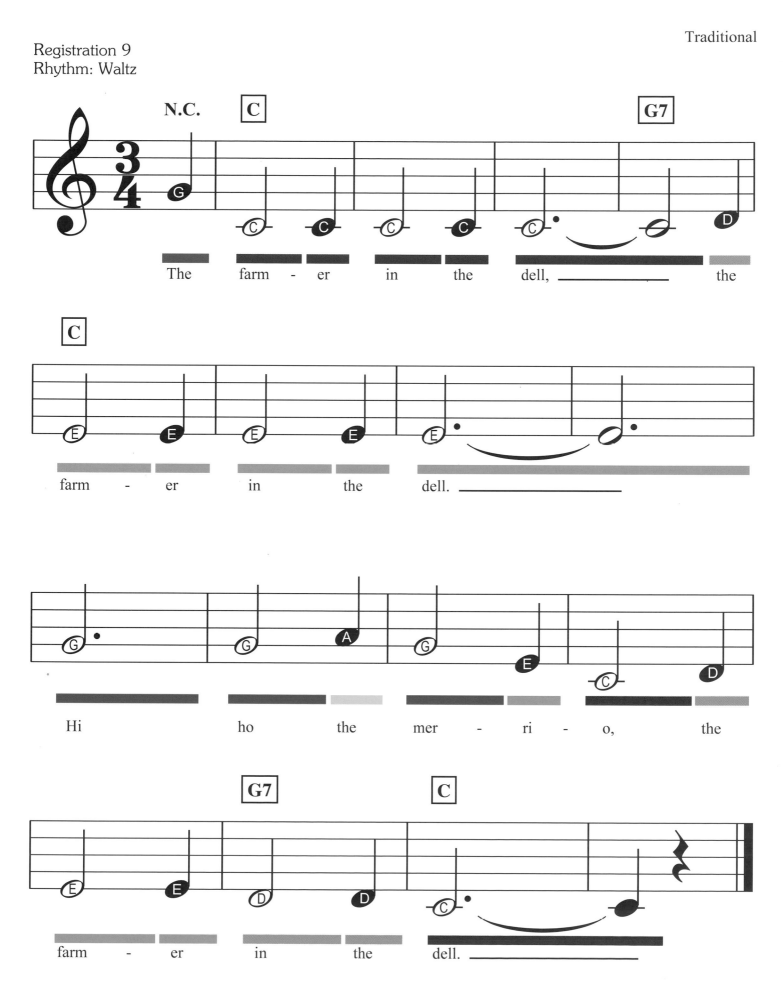

EENSY WEENSY SPIDER

Traditional

Registration 9
Rhythm: Waltz

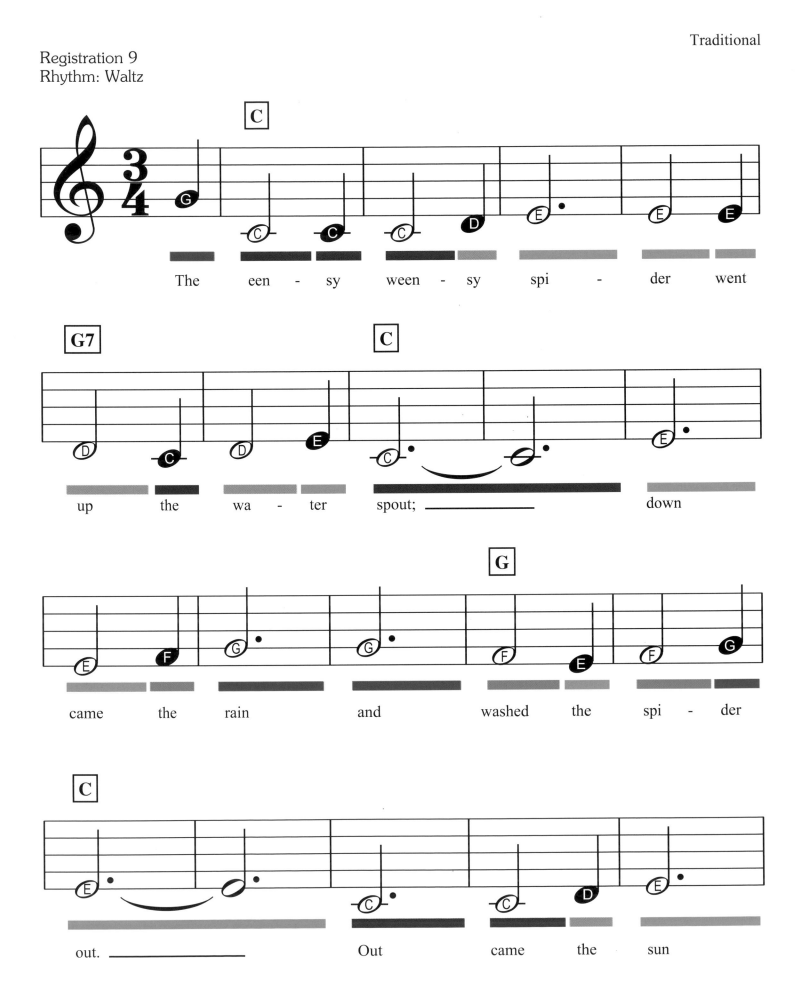

G7

C

and   dried   up   all   the   rain,   and   the

een - sy   ween - sy   spi - der   went

G7

C

up   the   spout   a - gain. _____

FOR HE'S A JOLLY GOOD FELLOW

Registration 9
Rhythm: Waltz

Traditional

FRÈRE JACQUES
(Are You Sleeping?)

Traditional

Registration 6
Rhythm: March

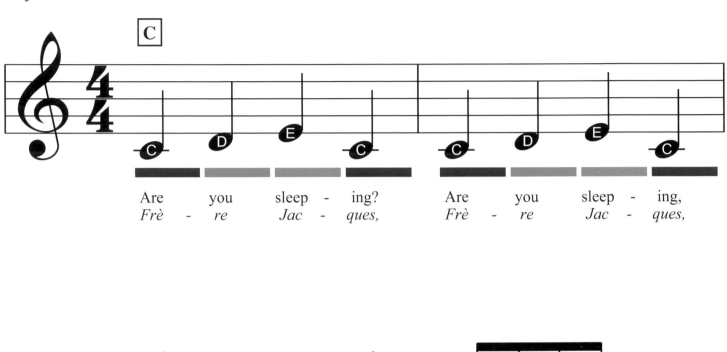

Are you sleep - ing? Are you sleep - ing,
Frè - re Jac - ques, Frè - re Jac - ques,

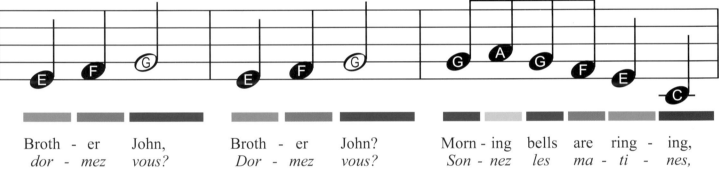

Broth - er John, Broth - er John? Morn - ing bells are ring - ing,
dor - mez vous? Dor - mez vous? Son - nez les ma - ti - nes,

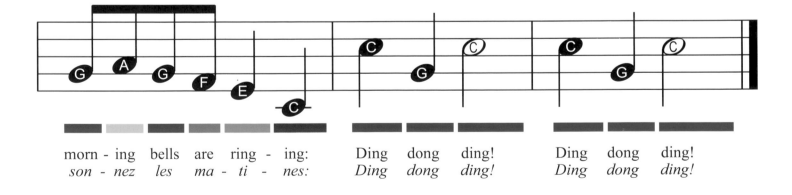

morn - ing bells are ring - ing: Ding dong ding! Ding dong ding!
son - nez les ma - ti - nes: Ding dong ding! Ding dong ding!

HICKORY DICKORY DOCK

Registration 10
Rhythm: Waltz

Traditional

HEY DIDDLE DIDDLE

Traditional

Registration 10
Rhythm: Waltz

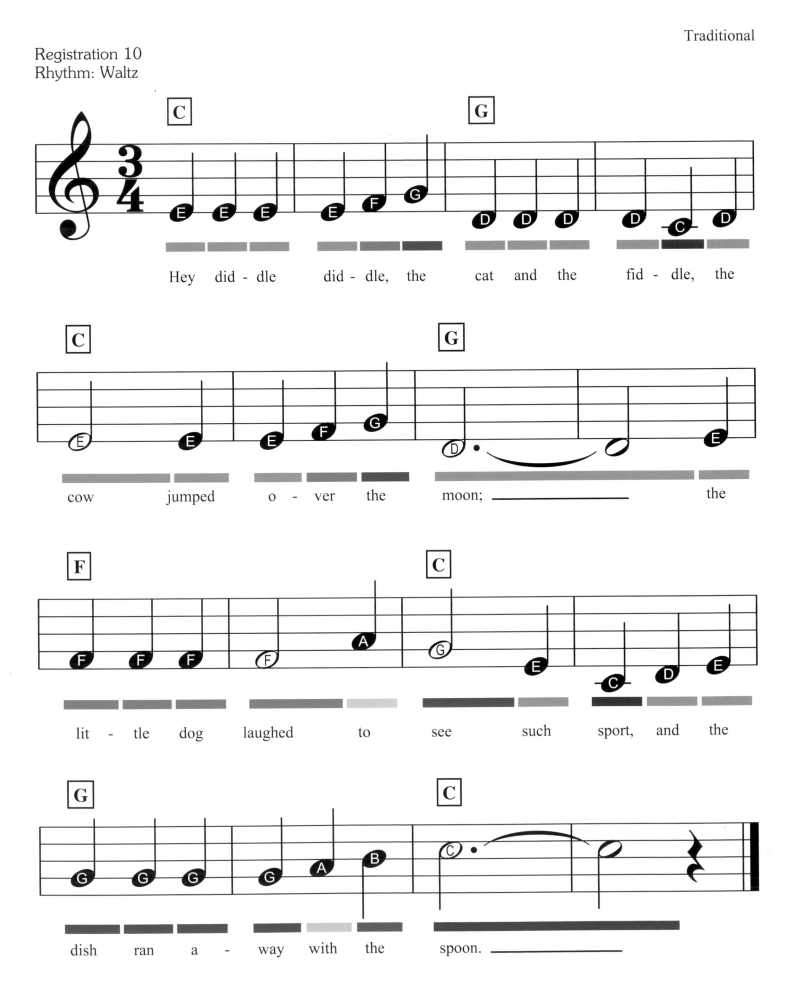

HUMPTY DUMPTY

Registration 4
Rhythm: Waltz

Traditional

JACK SPRAT

Registration 7
Rhythm: Fox Trot

Traditional

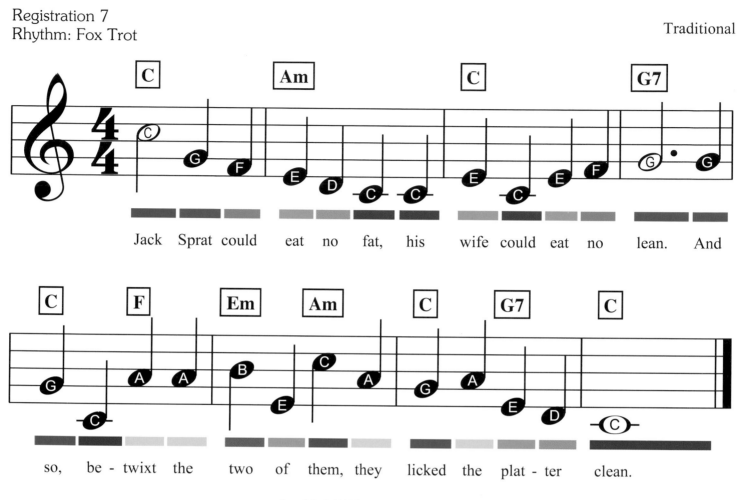

Jack Sprat could eat no fat, his wife could eat no lean. And

so, be - twixt the two of them, they licked the plat - ter clean.

I'VE BEEN WORKING ON THE RAILROAD

Registration 7
Rhythm: March or Fox Trot

American Folksong

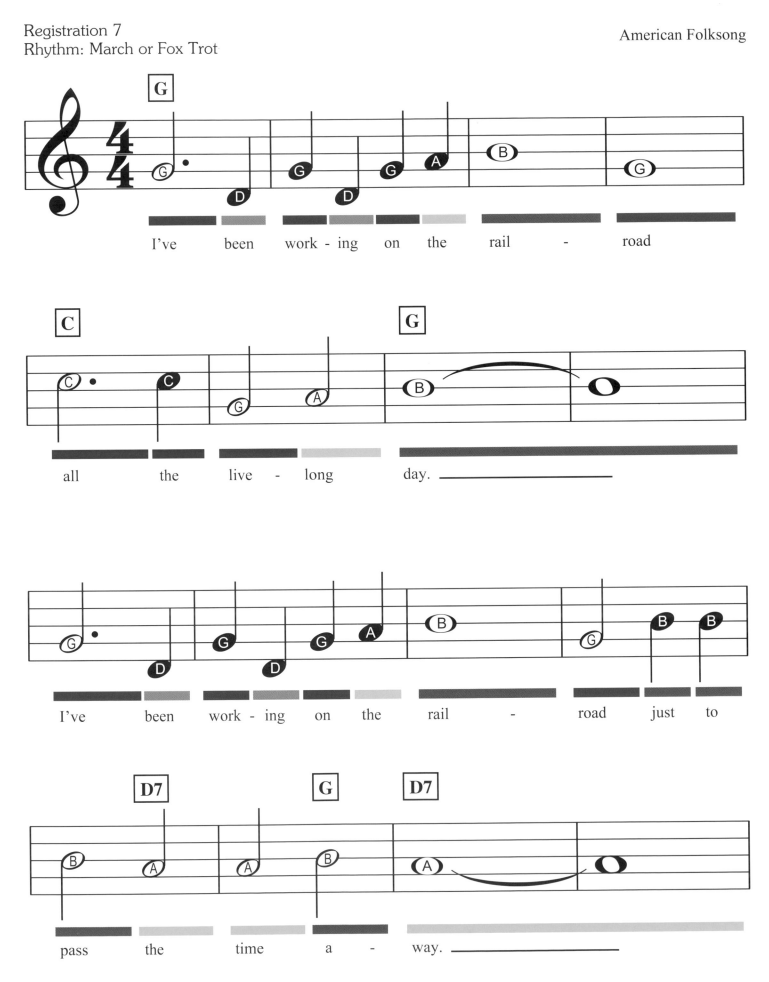

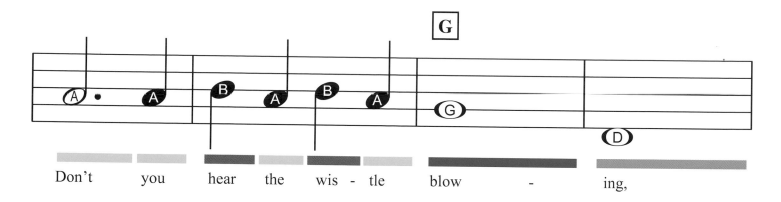

Don't you hear the wis - tle blow - ing,

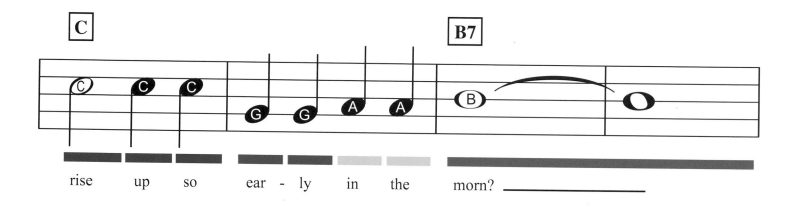

rise up so ear - ly in the morn? _____

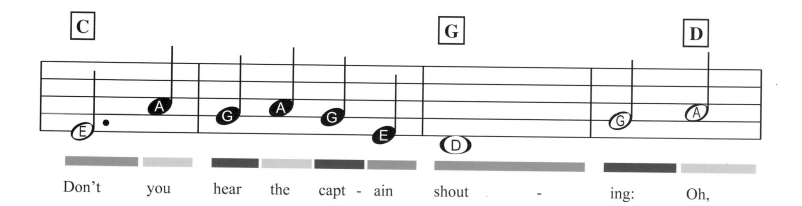

Don't you hear the capt - ain shout - ing: Oh,

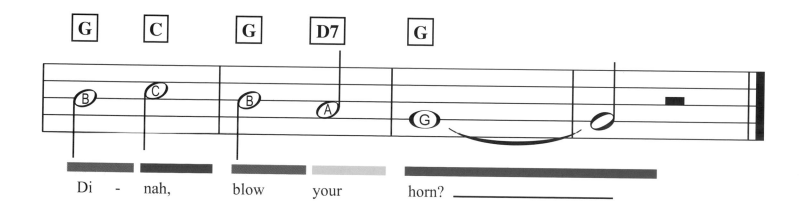

Di - nah, blow your horn? _____

JINGLE BELLS

Words and Music by
J. Pierpont

Registration 8
Rhythm: Swing or Fox Trot

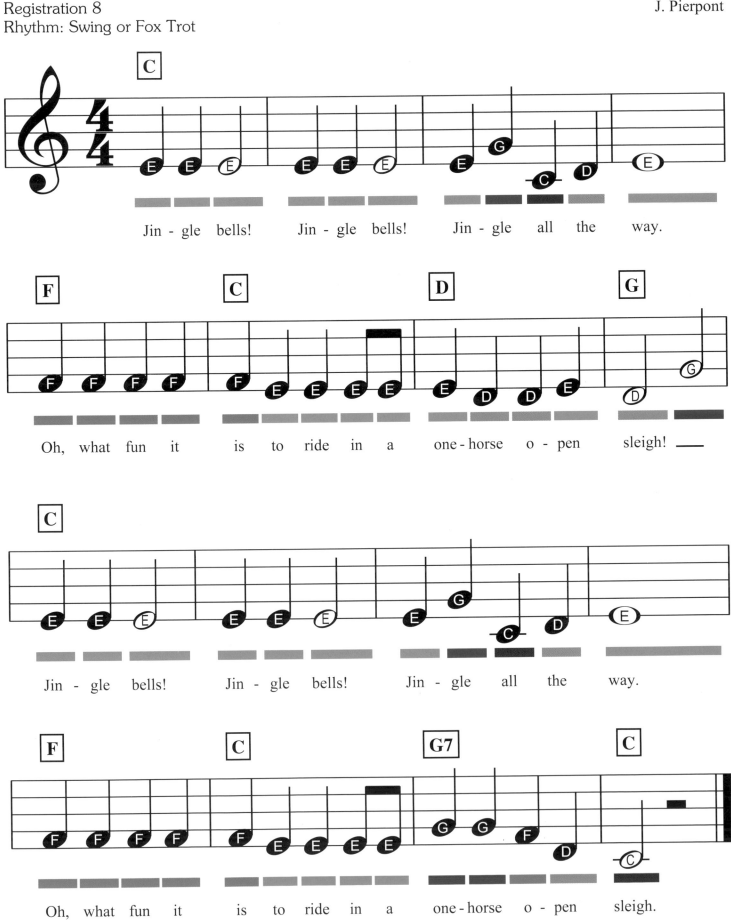

KUMBAYA

Congo Folksong

Registration 1
Rhythm: Ballad

2. Someone's praying, etc.
3. Someone's searching, etc.
4. Someone's giving, etc.
5. Someone's loving, etc.

6. Someone's hungry, etc.
7. Someone's dying, etc.
8. Someone's praising, etc.

LIGHTLY ROW

Traditional

Registration 1
Rhythm: March

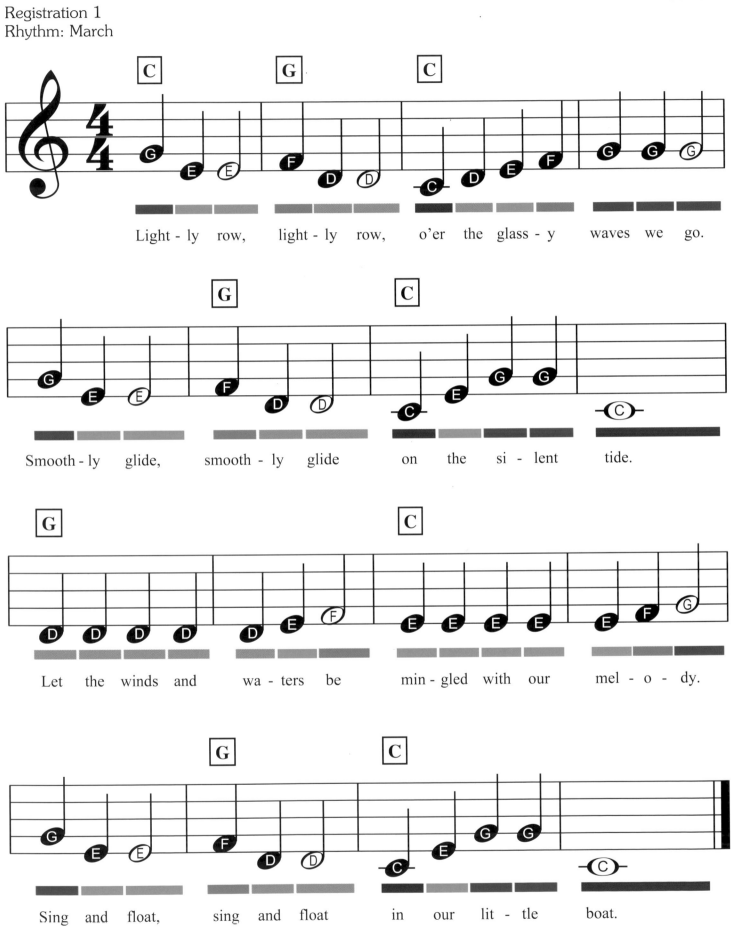

Can you find the hidden musical objects?

(Answers are on page 78.)

flat sign	violin	boom box	3 half notes
sharp sign	trumpet	guitar	saxophone
2 treble clef signs	piano keys	xylophone	quarter rest
drum	record	time signature $\frac{4}{4}$	repeat sign

LITTLE BO-PEEP

Registration 1
Rhythm: Waltz

Traditional

LONDON BRIDGE

Registration 1
Rhythm: Fox Trot

Traditional

1. Lon - don Bridge is fall - ing down, fall - ing down, fall - ing down.

Lon - don Bridge is fall - ing down, my fair la - dy.

2. Build it up with iron bars, iron bars, iron bars.
   Build it up with iron bars, my fair lady.

3. Iron bars will bend and break, bend and break, bend and break.
   Iron bars will bend and break, my fair lady.

4. Build it up with silver and gold, silver and gold, silver and gold.
   Build it up with silver and gold, my fair lady.

LONG, LONG AGO

Registration 1
Rhythm: Swing or Fox Trot

By Thomas Bayly

LULLABY

By Johannes Brahms

Registration 3
Rhythm: Waltz

THE MAN ON THE FLYING TRAPEZE

Words by George Leybourne
Music by Alfred Lee

Registration 9
Rhythm: Waltz

MUSICAL WORDS

There are many words that use just the seven letters of the musical alphabet. You might say they are "musical words." Here are some of them. Fill in the blanks below each note to make a musical word. In case you get stuck, there's a clue below each word.

After you've filled in the blanks, play each word to hear how it sounds musically. Also, try putting different words together to form complete "musical sentences" and then play them.

3-Letter Words

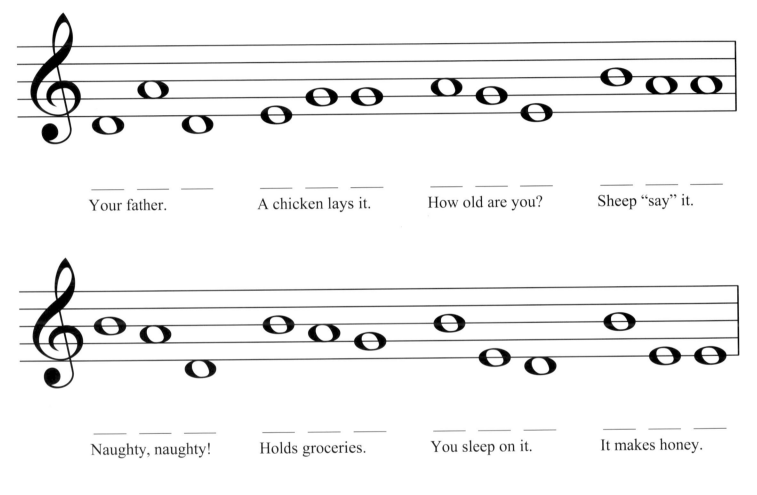

Your father.   A chicken lays it.   How old are you?   Sheep "say" it.

Naughty, naughty!   Holds groceries.   You sleep on it.   It makes honey.

4-Letter Words

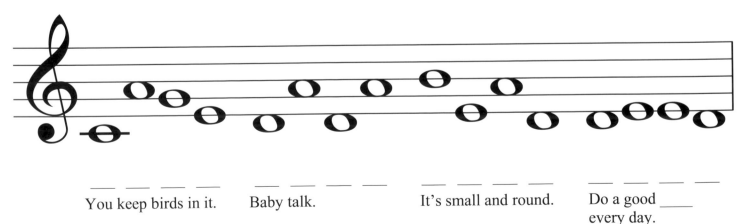

You keep birds in it.   Baby talk.   It's small and round.   Do a good _____ every day.

This page is a little tricky, because there are no hints to help you.
Fill in the note names to create a word, then check your answers on page 79.

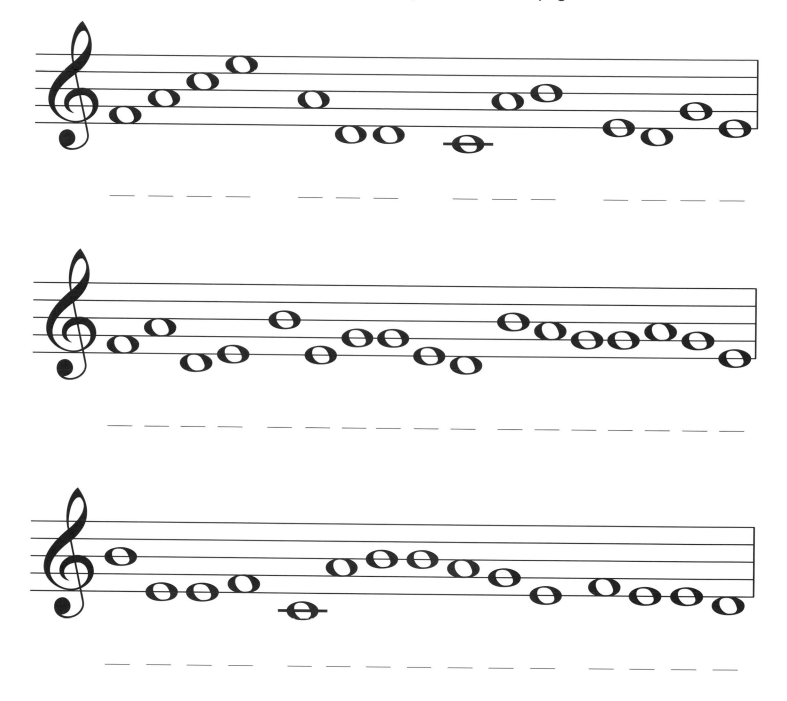

MARY HAD A LITTLE LAMB

Registration 7
Rhythm: Fox Trot

Words by Sarah Josepha Hale
Traditional Music

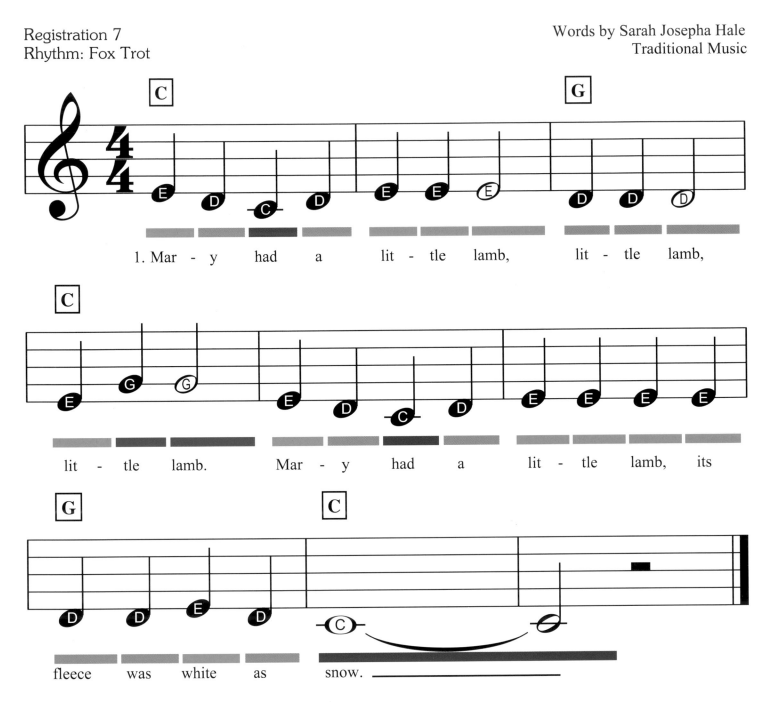

2. Ev'rywhere that Mary went, Mary went, Mary went,
   Ev'rywhere that Mary went the lamb was sure to go.

3. (It) followed her to school one day, school one day, school one day,
   (It) followed her to school one day, which was against the rule.

4. (It) made the children laugh and play, laugh and play, laugh and play,
   (It) made the children laugh and play to see a lamb at school.

5. (And) so the teacher turned him out, turned him out, turned him out,
   (And) so the teacher turned him out, but still he lingered near.

6. (And) waited patiently about, patiently, patiently,
   (And) waited patiently about till Mary did appear.

MICHAEL, ROW THE BOAT ASHORE

Traditional Folksong

Registration 4
Rhythm: Folk or Rock

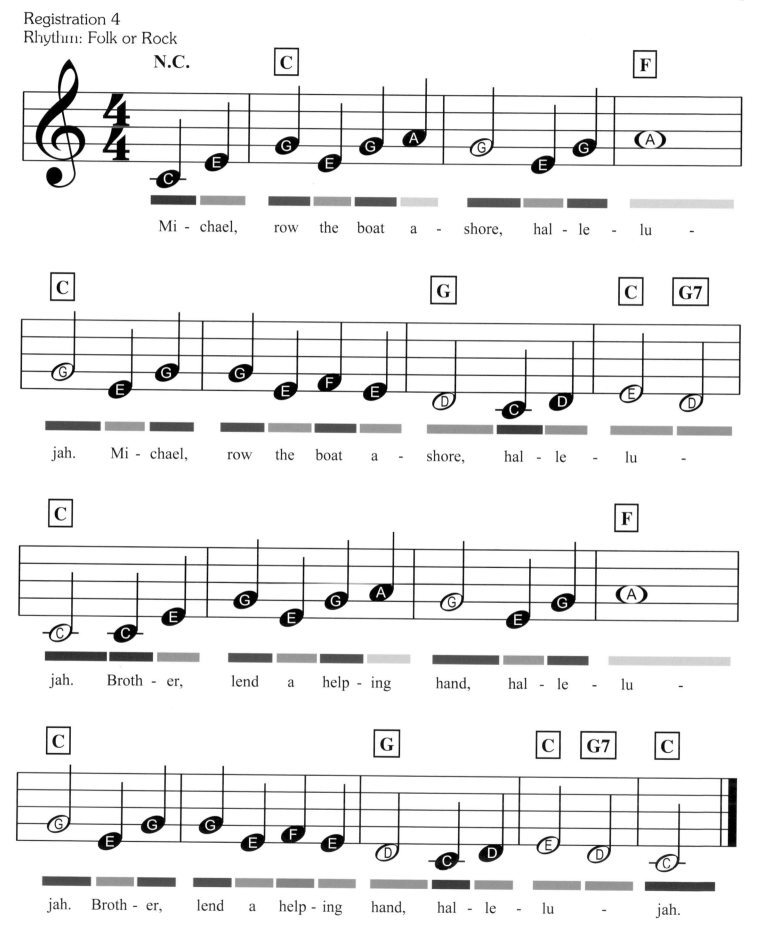

THE MULBERRY BUSH

Registration 9
Rhythm: Waltz

Traditional

NEW WORLD SYMPHONY
(Second Movement Theme)

Registration 3
Rhythm: Waltz or None

By Antonin Dvořák

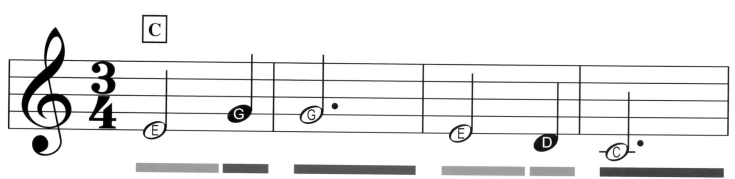

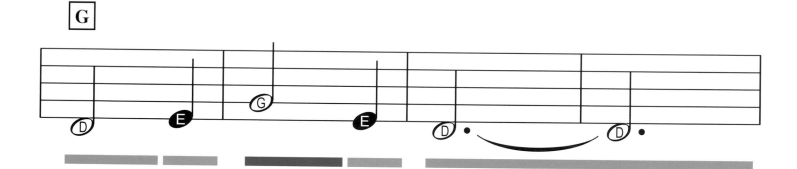

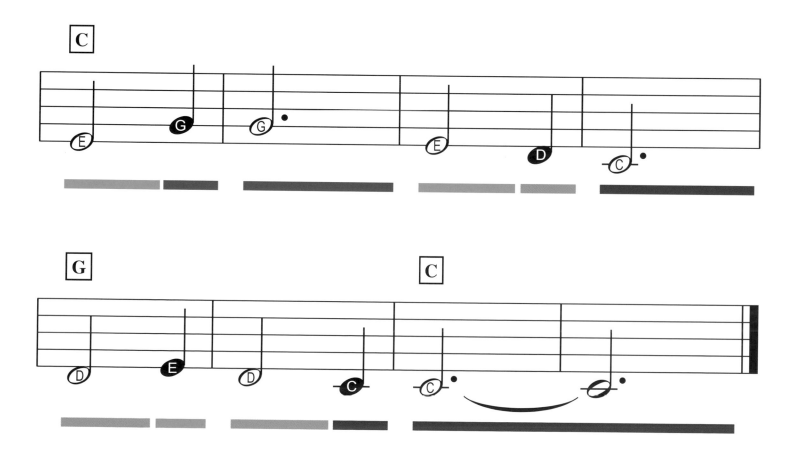

OH DEAR! WHAT CAN THE MATTER BE?

Registration 8
Rhythm: Waltz

Traditional

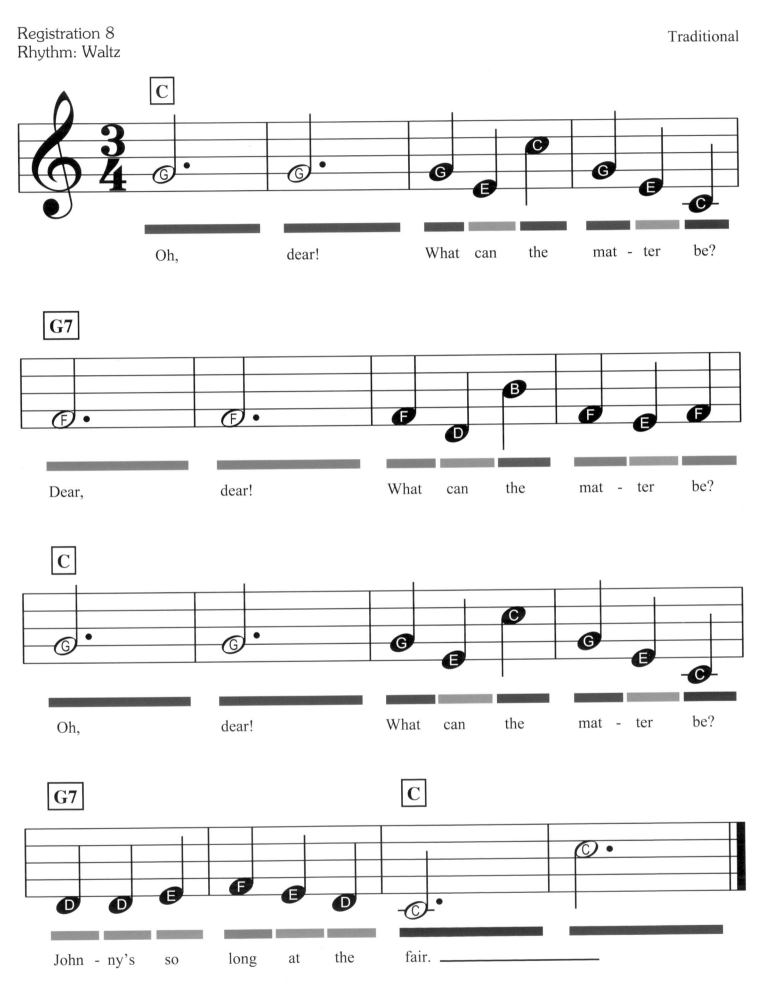

THE OLD GRAY MARE

Words and Music by
J. Warner

Registration 4
Rhythm: Swing

OH! SUSANNA

Words and Music by
Stephen C. Foster

Registration 4
Rhythm: Fox Trot

I _____ came from Al - a - bam - a with my

ban - jo on my knee. I'm goin' to Lou' - si -

an - a, my _____ true love for to see. It

rained all night the day I left, the weath - er it was

51

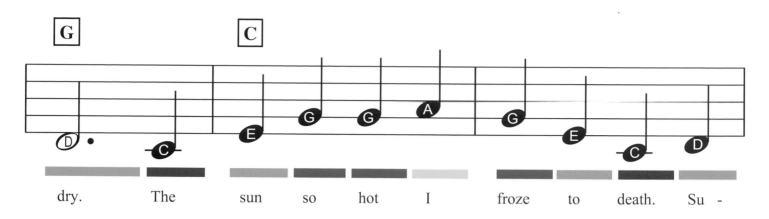

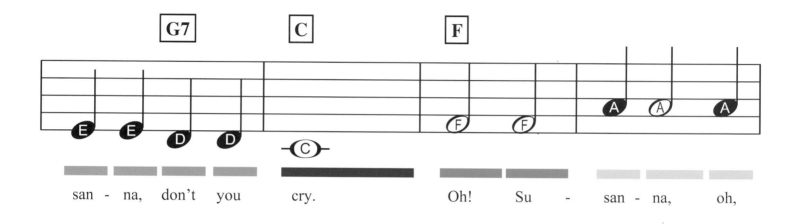

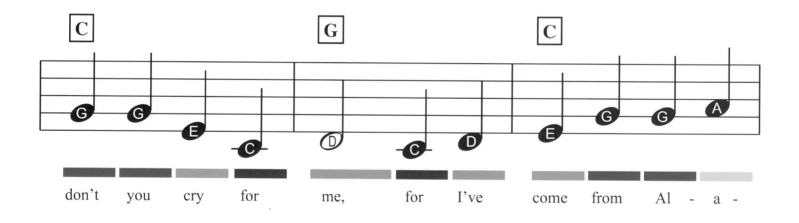

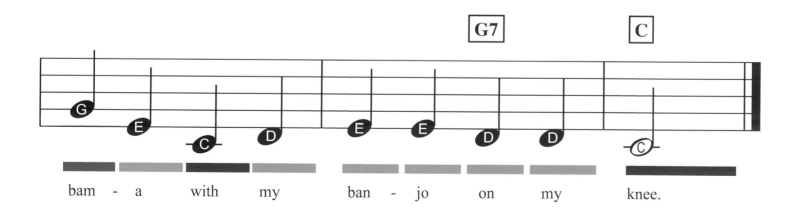

OLD MacDONALD

Traditional Children's Song

Registration 10
Rhythm: Fox Trot

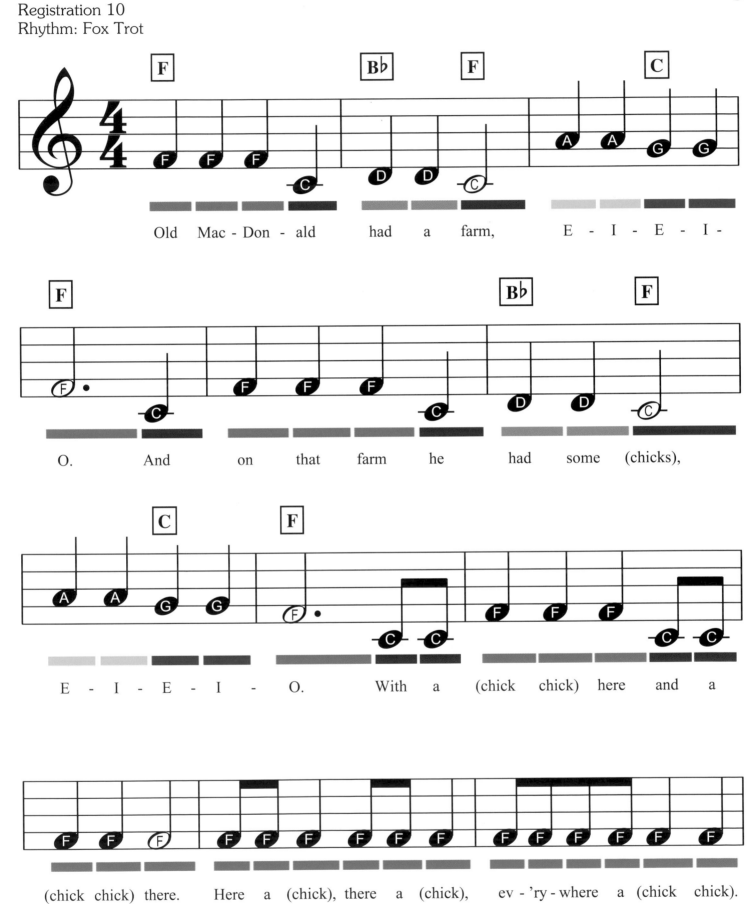

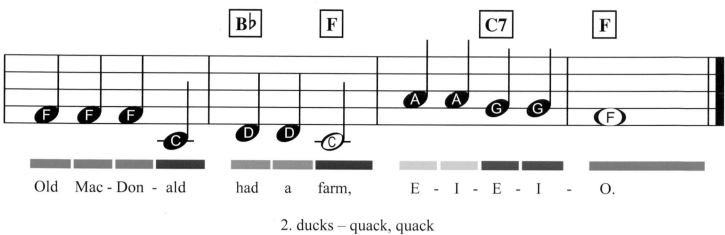

Old   Mac - Don - ald   had   a   farm,   E - I - E - I - O.

2. ducks – quack, quack
3. pigs – oink, oink
4. cows – moo, moo
5. sheep – baa, baa

ON TOP OF OLD SMOKY

Kentucky Mountain Folksong

Registration 4
Rhythm: Waltz

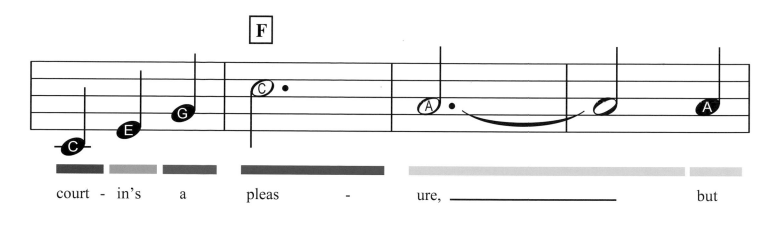

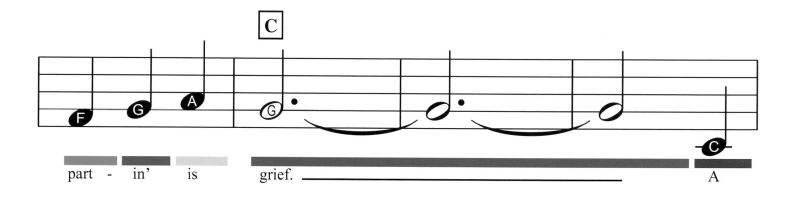

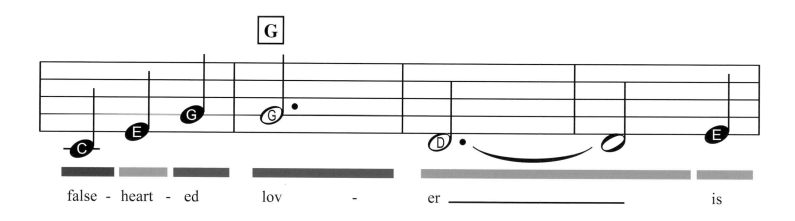

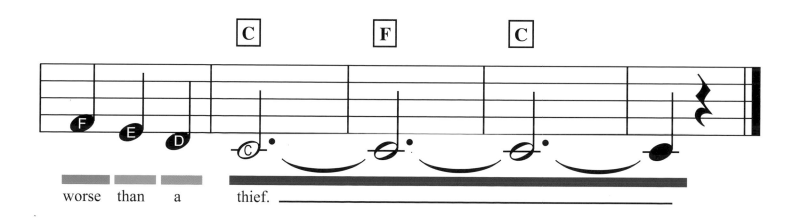

OVER THE RIVER
AND THROUGH THE WOODS

Registration 7
Rhythm: Waltz

Traditional

2.

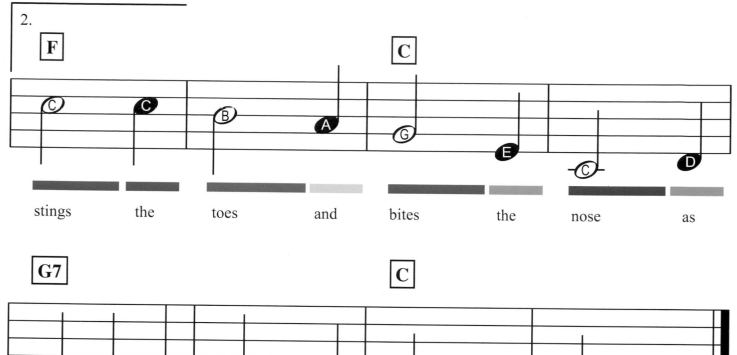

stings   the   toes   and   bites   the   nose   as

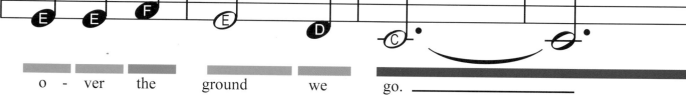

o - ver   the   ground   we   go. _____

POP GOES THE WEASEL

Registration 9
Rhythm: Waltz

Traditional

RAIN, RAIN, GO AWAY

Registration 1
Rhythm: Fox Trot

Traditional

ROW, ROW, ROW YOUR BOAT

Registration 7
Rhythm: Waltz

Traditional

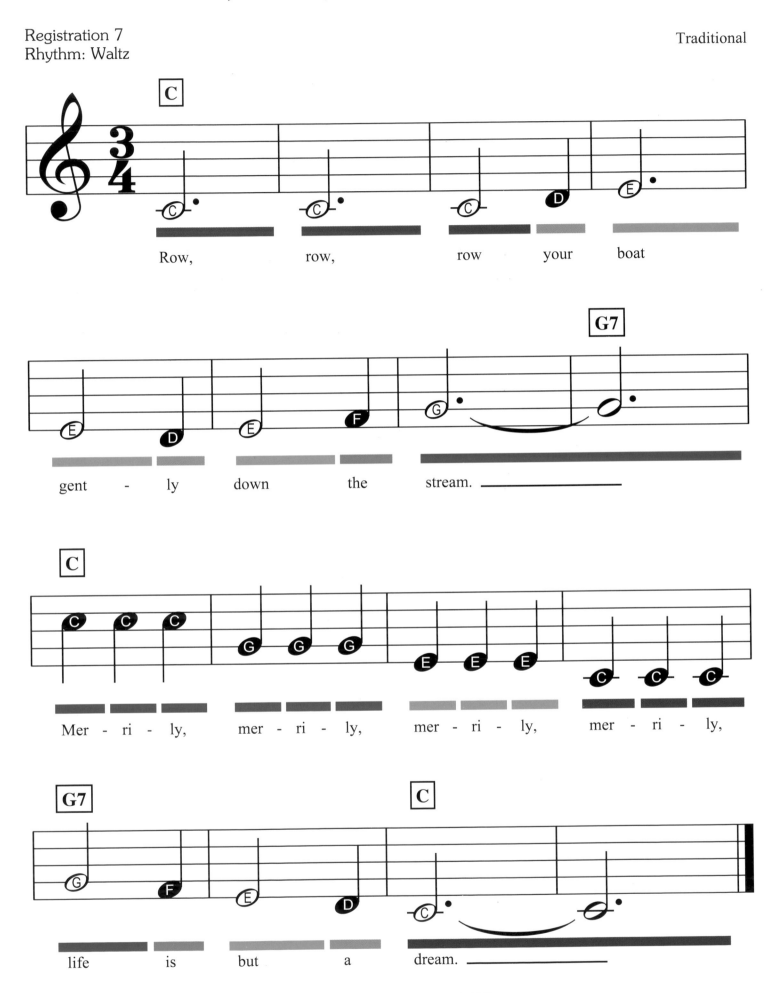

REUBEN AND RACHEL

Words and Music by
Harry Birch

Registration 8
Rhythm: Fox Trot

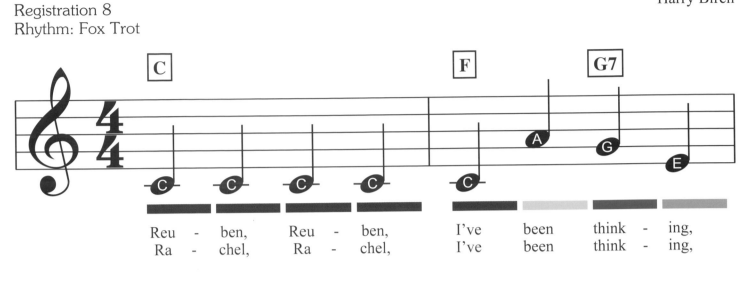

Reu - ben, Reu - ben, I've been think - ing,
Ra - chel, Ra - chel, I've been think - ing,

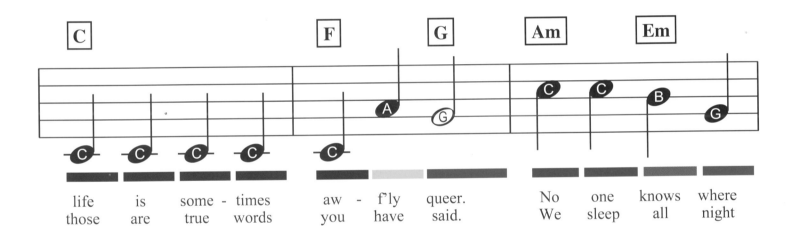

life is some - times aw - f'ly queer. No one knows where
those are true words you have said. We sleep all night

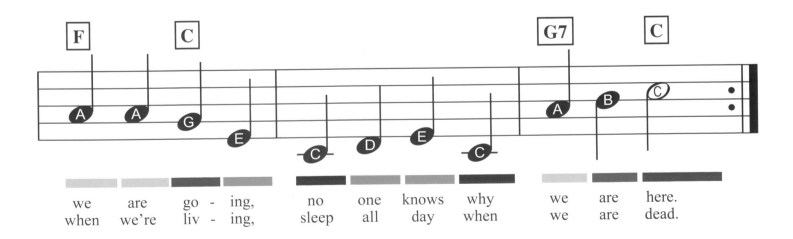

we are go - ing, no one knows why we are here.
when we're liv - ing, sleep all day when we are dead.

SAKURA
(Cherry Blossoms)

Registration 8
Rhythm: Ballad or 8-Beat

Traditional Japanese Folksong

SING A SONG OF SIXPENCE

Traditional

Registration 7
Rhythm: Swing

Sing a song of six - pence, a pock - et full of rye.

Four and twen - ty black - birds baked in a pie.

When the pie was o - pened, the birds be - gan to sing.

Was - n't that a dain - ty dish to set be - fore the king? _____

This exercise is fun and will help you to identify musical signs. Just draw a line from each musical term to the picture that matches the term.

(Answers are found on page 80.)

eighth note

quarter note

half note

dotted half note

whole note

quarter rest

half rest

whole rest

treble clef sign

tie

bar line

repeat sign

sharp sign

flat sign

chord symbol

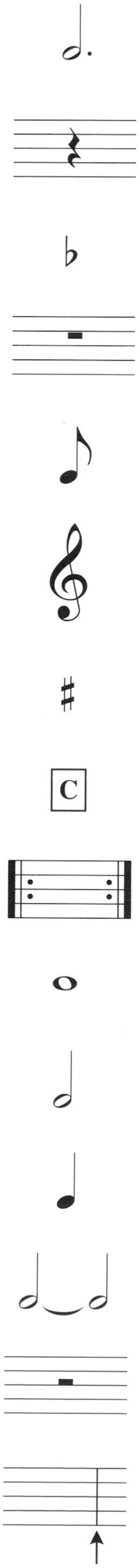

SKYE BOAT SONG

Registration 8
Rhythm: Waltz

Words by ROBERT LOUIS STEVENSON
Traditional Scottish Melody

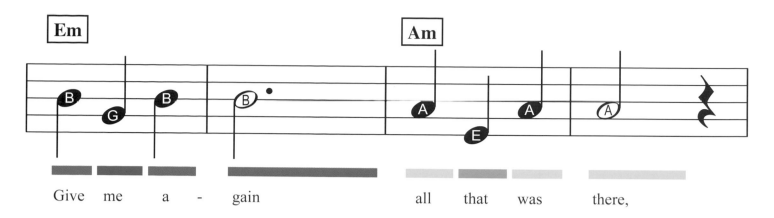

Em | Am

Give me a - gain   all that was there,

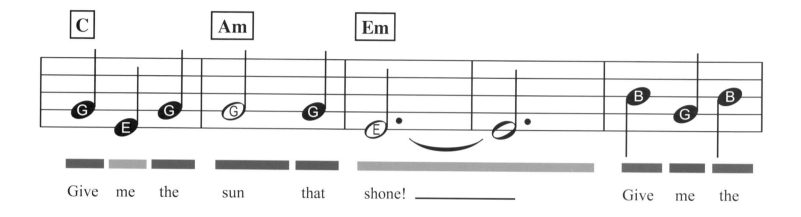

C | Am | Em

Give me the sun that shone! _____   Give me the

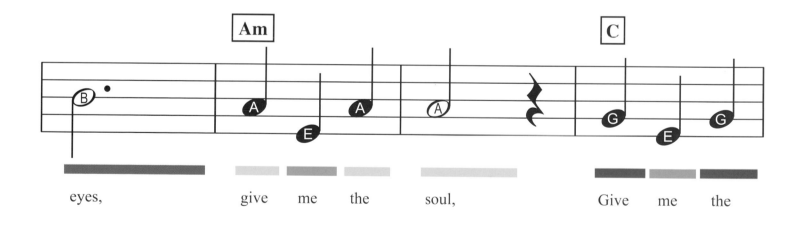

Am | C

eyes,   give me the soul,   Give me the

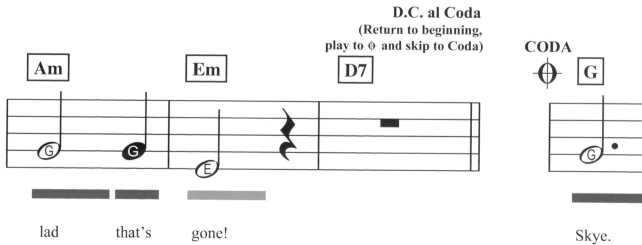

D.C. al Coda
(Return to beginning,
play to ⊕ and skip to Coda)

Am | Em | D7

lad that's gone!

CODA

⊕ | G

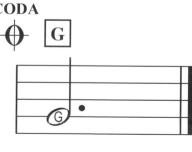

Skye.

TAKE ME OUT TO THE BALL GAME

Words by Jack Norworth
Music by Albert von Tilzer

Registration 7
Rhythm: Waltz

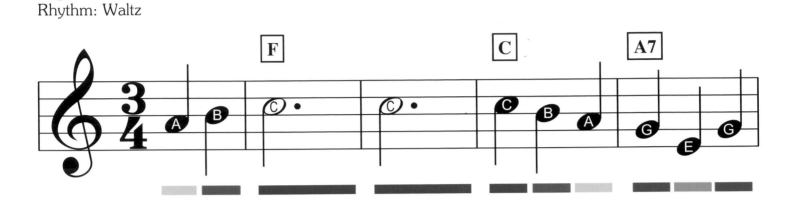

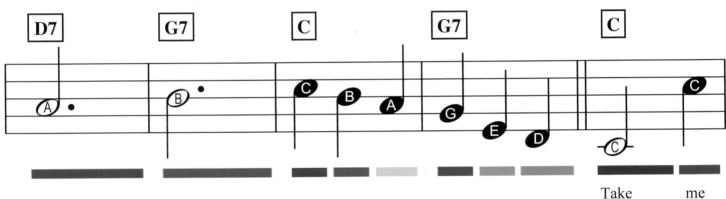

Take me

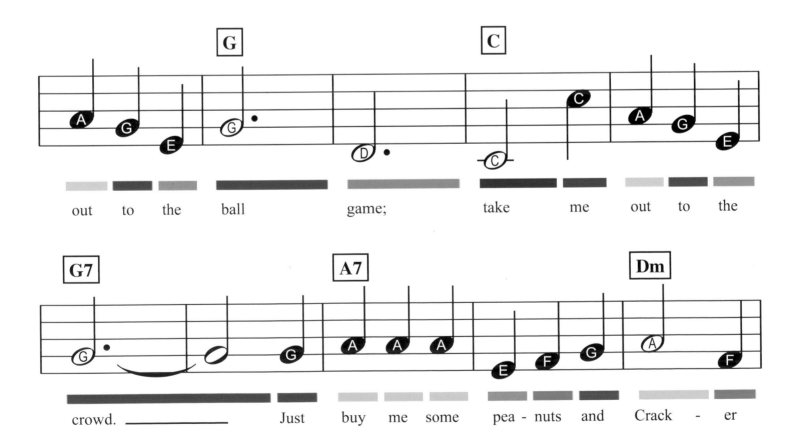

out   to   the   ball   game;   take   me   out   to   the

crowd. _____   Just   buy   me   some   pea - nuts   and   Crack - er

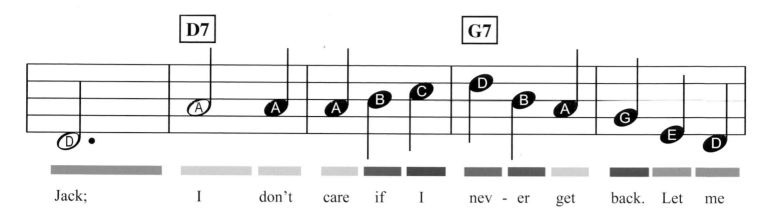

Jack; I don't care if I nev - er get back. Let me

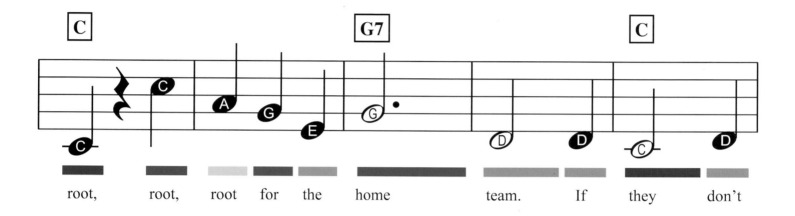

root, root, root for the home team. If they don't

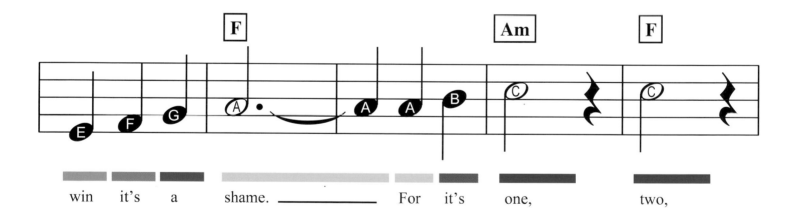

win it's a shame. _____ For it's one, two,

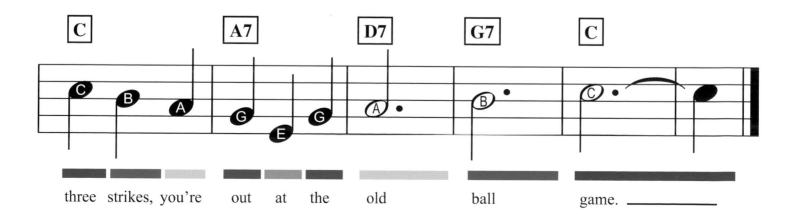

three strikes, you're out at the old ball game. _____

THIS OLD MAN

Traditional

Registration 5
Rhythm: March

1. This old man, he played one, he played knick - knack on his thumb. With a knick - knack pad - dy - whack, give the dog a bone, this old man came roll - ing home.

2. This old man, he played two, he played knick-knack on his shoe, etc.
3. This old man, he played three, he played knick-knack on his knee, etc.
4. This old man, he played four, he played knick-knack on his door, etc.
5. This old man, he played five, he played knick-knack on this hive, etc.
6. This old man, he played six, he played knick-knack on these bricks, etc.
7. This old man, he played sev'n, he played knick-knack on this ov'n, etc.
8. This old man, he played eight, he played knick-knack on this gate, etc.
9. This old man, he played nine, he played knick-knack on this line, etc.
10. This old man, he played ten, he played knick-knack on this hen, etc.

TWINKLE, TWINKLE, LITTLE STAR

Traditional

Registration 1
Rhythm: Ballad or Fox Trot

72

THREE BLIND MICE

Traditional

Registration 9
Rhythm: Waltz

C	G	C

E • D • C • C

Three blind mice, _____

G	C	G

E • D • C • C G •

Three blind mice. _____ See

C	G

F F E • E G • F F

how they run, _____ See how they

C		G	C

E • E G C C B A B C G

run. _____ They all ran af - ter the farm - er's

UP ON THE HOUSETOP

Registration 8
Rhythm: Swing

Words and Music by
B.R. Hanby

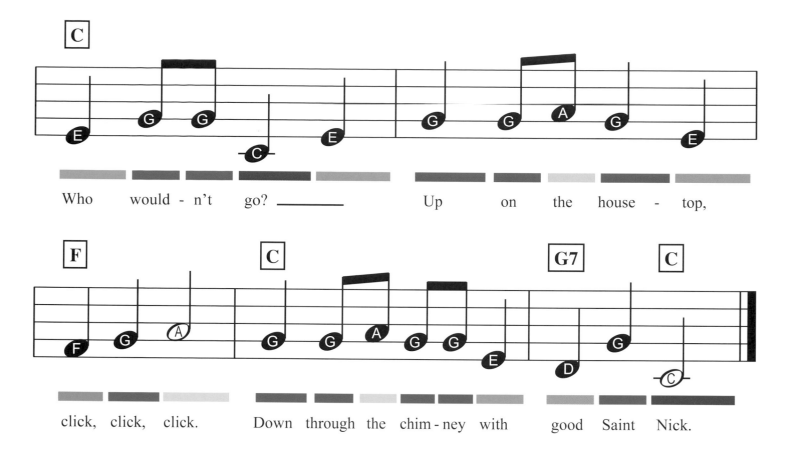

C

Who would-n't go? ———— Up on the house-top,

F **C** **G7** **C**

click, click, click. Down through the chim-ney with good Saint Nick.

YANKEE DOODLE

Traditional

Registration 2
Rhythm: March

C   F

A B C   G A G F   E G   A B A G

keep   it   up!   Yank - ee   Doo - dle   dan - dy!   Mind   the   mu - sic

C   G7   C

A B C A   G C B D   C C

and   the   step,   and   with   the   girls   be   han - dy!

(Page 35)

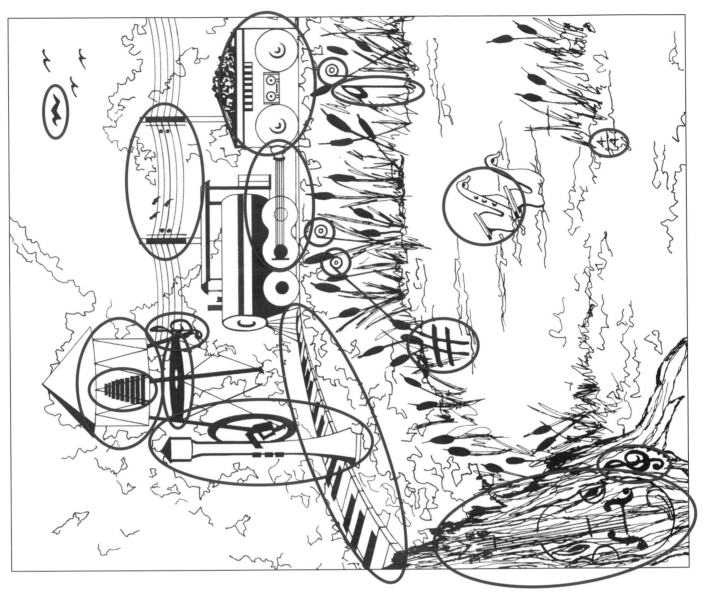

(Page 15)

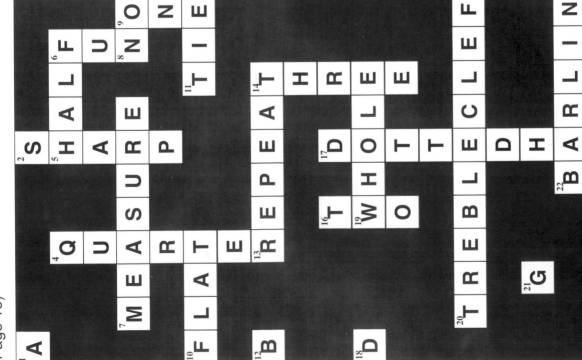

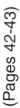

(Pages 42-43)

3-Letter Words

4-Letter Words

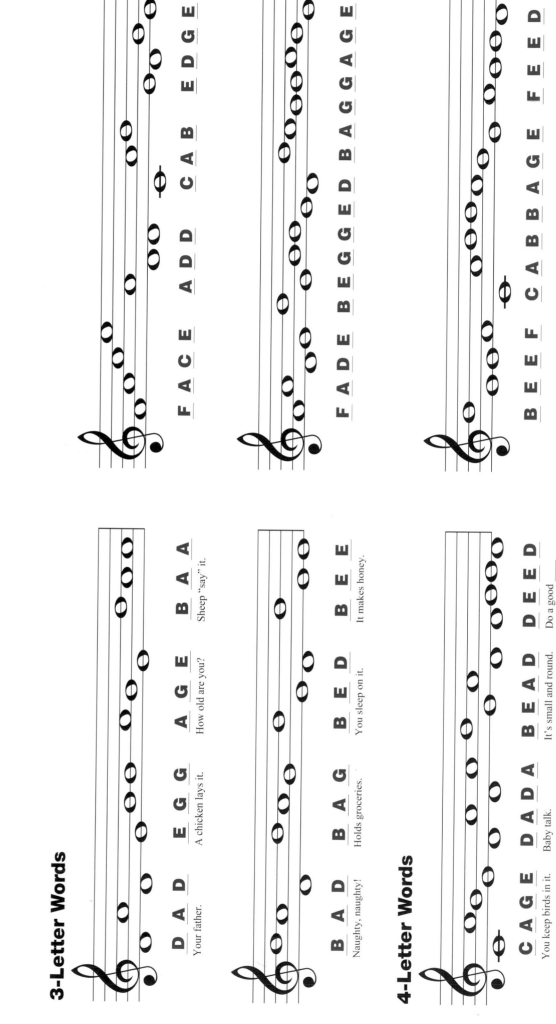

D A D
Your father.

E G G
A chicken lays it.

A G E
How old are you?

B A A
Sheep "say" it.

B A D
Naughty, naughty!

B A G
Holds groceries.

B E D
You sleep on it.

B E E
It makes honey.

C A G E
You keep birds in it.

D A D A
Baby talk.

B E A D
It's small and round.

D E E D
Do a good
every day.

F A C E

A D D

C A B

E D G E

F A D E

B E G G E D

B A G G A G E

B E E F

C A B B A G E

F E E D

80

(Page 65)

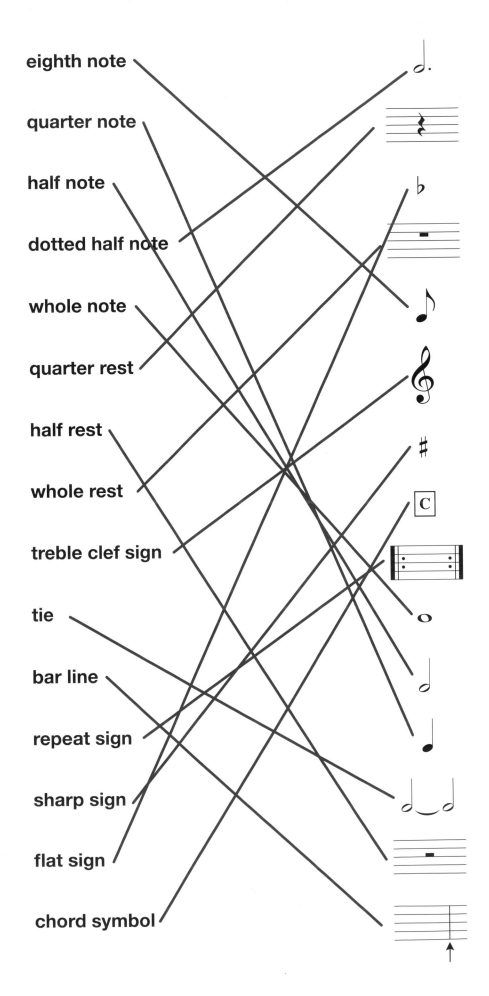